Not Of This

This

M.M. Bylo

Printed in the United States of America
First edition, April 2025

Cover design by M.M. Bylo

ISBN (paperback): 979-8-9893483-3-6

www.mmbylo.com
marissabylo@gmail.com

To the "weird" ones.
Go enjoy life and how you were created to be.
That's the sweetest revenge there is.

Contents

Part 3: God

Part 1

Dear Me, Myself, And I

Healing Out Loud

If you're looking for a getaway
        Slip on rose-colored glasses
        Drink until life blurs
        Blame the stars and planets
        For your shortfalls
        Hang skeletons in your closet
        Dance to this self-destructive rhythm
You're in the wrong place

We walk on the shattered glass
Of our lives
Feel our pain
Fight uphill battles
Trudge through the trenches
        To heal
        To learn
        To teach

If you're looking for excuses
You won't find them here.

Ambition's Dark Side

I called myself
        Ambitious
Because it sounded pleasant
Empowering
And society celebrates
Status and exhaustion
Don't they

But the mirror doesn't deceive—
        Avoidance
        Impatience
        Insecurity
Stared back at me
Their eyes hungry
And stomachs empty

No matter what I do
It will never be
Enough for them
Will it?

Patience, Grasshopper

All the doors I ran toward
Clawing at them
In my own strength
Fixated and obsessed

When any door swung open
Each red flag waving madly
It's no wonder
That I crashed and burned

Only to shut it slowly
Swaddled in regret
And laid outside
In shambles

Lamenting—
I should have *stopped*
Listened
And *waited.*

In Memoriam

My entire life spent
Trying to prove to them and myself—
       I could ace their tests
       Exceed expectations
       Fit their crafted mold
       Save the world from itself

But like a candle
Alight at both ends
This zeal had nowhere to rest
I burned myself out
And no one knew
What to do with my ashes.

Small Talk

I was running everyone's race
Except the one marked for me
Failing miserably
Criticizing myself to no end

And if they should question
What's new in my life
Only one response
Feels sincere to utter—

I'm no longer hustling
For things that aren't meant for me.

My Civil Disobedience

I showed the populace
I could pass their tests
But lost myself in the process
This race they created
Only winners and losers

But I tasted something sweeter
A slower, intentional life
I defied expectations
And stopped to smell
The flowers.

Casually Countercultural

To be still
To reflect
To appreciate
To wait
To forgive
To be grateful
To abide
In the present
To listen
Without a reply
To feel feelings
As they arrive

How lovely
And rebellious.

Powerless

Society's tireless mantras—
        Believe in yourself
        Deny any weakness
        Strive until you die
        Work hard enough
        And you'll achieve
        All your desires
The poster child for that
Threadbare life
I collapsed and discovered
My strength's expiration date

But maybe feeling powerless
Is the lesson
The truth
I needed all along.

Liberation

I couldn't save the world
I couldn't even save myself
And that somehow—
Ironically—
Freed me.

In Defense Of My New Rhythm

If overcompensation
       Never ceasing
Busybody
       No respite
Neglecting rest
       Hurried feet
Running ahead
       Without restraints
       Or wisdom
Brought me to this place
Why should I believe
Repeating history
Would bring the healing
And blessings
That I need?

Sweet Creature

Tasted humanity's poison
But refused to surrender
To their bitterness and cruelty
Weighing them down
Like invisible chains
She took verbal assassinations
Without retaliation
Sensitivity became strength
Empathy, her armor
Mercy, her guide
As she chose the higher road
Time after time
No good ever occurred
From recycling hatred
So sweet she shall be
Until the flesh forfeits.

Tender

I used to be like a firework
Even if they didn't like the view
At least they'd hear me
And pay attention

But once the performance ended
They'd inevitably depart
No longer amused
I was a spectacle of my own doing

I want to be a hearth ablaze
Warm and inviting
Without expecting recompense
To burn when they don't notice

Or choose not to remain
To be a source of comfort
Then left alone
When time decides

Fire tenders exist
And those who need to stick around
Will find their way
To me

I don't need to beg
I just need to be.

Gated Community

I've stared over the barricade
Of the gated community
For as long as I can recall
Wanting to be like them
Understood and accepted
Into their elusive exclusivity

I tried on different costumes
And after much practice
They seemed to tolerate
My ambition
Conformity
Selflessness they could manipulate

But no matter the performance
Shame never found its rest
I overcompensated
Until I imploded
And every crafted mask
Clattered to the floor

There will always be someone
With a disapproving glare
Their words like swords
Poised to annihilate
Even with their fickle praise
Self-acceptance begins within

Shame can't live here
When you understand
Where your value originates
Look up, child
You were worth loving
All along.

If Survival Is Insufficient

Then tell me
What is living

Perhaps—

      Dancing alone in a galley kitchen
      Slick wooden floors below woolen socks
      Punk rock rattling space and atoms

Cinnamon-sprinkled, honey-slathered fried apples
Belly laughs and reddened cheeks
A kiss no one sees

      Twin giggles bringing levity
      Food everywhere but a mouth
      Longings of what the future could hold

      (Who but God knows)

Holidays surrounded by kin
Flames flickering in their place
Memories playing out on the television

      Stringed instruments
      Fan blades oscillating
      Illumination at the flick of a finger

All the things
I take for granted
Still within my reach

This is living—

Even the delirious evenings
Cold presses cradling a forehead
Consumed by pain

This night will pass
As it always does

It always does
I assure myself again.

Sweet Revenge

The most rebellious act
I've ever committed
Was to keep living.

Who Had It Better: The Tortoise Or The Hare?

Life isn't a race
Each soul traverses
A unique path
Set before them
But why can't I shake
The impression
The dread
That I'm being left behind
In the dust
Of this infertile, cracked land?

Pillar Of Salt

Teach my heart
To enjoy the memories
But refrain from wanting
To return to those times
Nostalgia an intangible thing
Because what I miss
Is no longer there
Just here
Lingering in my mind
For the present
At a glance
Appears ominous
And the past
Always so rosy
Despite its thorns.

The Former Things

Forget what lies behind
I've nothing to return to
I know that much
But the road ahead curves
Into sheer nothingness
That terrifies
My inner child
And present self

I've always needed a road map
To live this life
Assurances and directions
Am I the only one
Who doesn't know
What they're doing anymore
Everyone seems certain
While I circle this plateau

I've been a selfish
Daughter, wife, and friend
Regrets accumulating
How do I stop them
From dragging me
Into disappointment's depths
These struggles aren't exclusive
But I can't seem to shake—

All the ghosts and hounds
That won't leave me
In peace but rather
In pieces.

Nothing's New

Ignoring the dissonance in my mind
The taunting lies—
     It won't get any better than this
But when I look around me
I can't help but echo the pessimism

Does *this* get any better

One step forward
Two backward
And a tumble
I grasp for progress
While defeat laughs above me

Where do I go from *here*

Facedown in the dirt
Despair clutching my ankles
Begging to be companions
I don't have the resolve
To resist her advances

I need nothing short
Of a miracle.

When Feelings Become Dictators

Shame points its talons
Curled fingers accusing me—
Still childless
College diplomas
Gather dust in some chest
Bursting with memories
And people long gone

Where did I go wrong
Every scheme ending
In vacant rooms
Omnipresent silence
And a petrified heart

Forge a new path, I'm told
Yet terror accompanies me
Each step forward
I have a habit
Of breaking, burning
And ruining
Everything given to me

I conceal that remorse
In the depths of my soul
A fist around my throat
Gnawing within my gut
A weight I can't relinquish

How do I acknowledge
My feelings
Without them
Controlling me
Like a marionette?

Fork In The Road

Chockful of regret and insecurity
Failure's unyielding chokehold
On my decisions and dreams
      I lie there
      At the two diverged paths
      Paralyzed
      As fellow travelers
      Step around my body
      Left behind
      Frozen in time
Curled into myself
From the fear
      With evidence
      With receipts
I didn't make this up
Or imagine it
It was all me

You'll have to lift me
Out of this mire
Strengthen these limbs
To live another day—
I can't do this without You.

Survivor's Guilt

I stayed busy
To stay alive
I remained here
Cleaving to
Such ruinous entities—
        Fear
        Disguised pride
        And sheer selfishness
These vices forsake me
One after another
I cling to the threads
Of the frayed life
I've sown
So be gentle
With my restless nature
And timid heart
I never thought
I'd make it this far
I never dreamed
What future
I could hold

Of all the people
Who left too soon
Why was I spared—
Is that me or the guilt speaking?

Stage Of Grief: Denial

Someone please answer—
How do you comfort
The idealist who found failure
At the end of that yellow brick road

How do you resuscitate
A dreamer spiraling further
        Still
In the nightmare that won't end

Balance is the key
To tiptoe that tightrope
But she's never been one
To shy from extremes

To let the dreamer down
And let her rise again
I'm only asking
For a friend.

Faithful Companion

Hope is cruel
To a calloused soul
At first touch

But against the odds
It pulls me
Back to my feet

Again—
And again—
And again.

Part 2

To Whom It May Concern

I Wrote This Instead Of Checking In On You

In the springtime we disappeared
Instead of blooming—
       I beneath torment's thumb
       As you fought to stay alive
We emerged
To behold the summer sun
Both wearied
Bruised and weathered
But breathing
Miraculously alive
And we'll beat on
Against life's cruel current
Reaching for that green light
Just beyond our fingertips
Until God calls us upward
And we taste the freedom
We always desired.

We Won't Forget

You've sunk low
But you rose high
To catch a breath
Another breeze caressing your skin
As a sunset paints its canvas
Stars and planets pinprick
The darkened cosmos beyond

You are miraculous
Even amidst the battle
When smoke's scent lingers
And you're plagued with scars
Only you can view
I'm proud of us
And you should be too.

Dry Bones

They exemplified
Hustle and achievement
But neglected to demonstrate—
       How to rest without guilt
       Rejuvenate
       Be comfortable and content
       In your own skin
Why are we surprised
We're but skeletons
Smoky, blackened bones
Burned out from expectations
Then accused
       For not trying harder
       And pushing through
Like all the other
Bitter, withered humanity
That came before us.

Thick Skin Didn't Make Me A Better Person

Are good intentions enough
If my words slice like knives
Does it matter if I'm right
While you're bleeding
From my sharpened tongue

Empathy and good manners
Lost themselves
In the pain and its echo
Years of memorizing
These four lonely walls

Excuses don't justify
This anger taken out
On another victim
Of my own depravity—
Forgive me

Seems my trials
Turned me mean.

Better Late Than Never

We aren't running the same race
We don't want the same things
Can you blame me
For constructing boundaries

To save us both
From my self-destructive patterns—
        Giving too much
        Or far too little

It's about time
I learned my lesson.

It's Complicated

You didn't know
How to love me
When I needed support
But I'm not without stain
I built barbed wire
Around my fractured life
And dared you to come in

You weren't made
To stay in my trenches
Nor I for your everyday life
Only here for a season
I must concede
Your company
That met its conclusion

Perhaps this sort of goodbye
Doesn't need words
Spoken out loud.

What Fair Weather

They want pumpkin spice
And all that's nice
But I'm searching for sparks and fire
Iron sharpening iron
Conversations dipping, diving
Below small talk's surface
And pleasantries
To the honest deep
Where we face our fears
Then come up to breathe

The reason I've gone silent—
        I have nothing new
        To say of the weather.

Breaker

Where are you now
Perhaps steeped in apathy
Because you've been saved
Have you fallen complacent
In your miraculous freedom

Forgotten your origin story
The mountain of impossibility
Split before your eyes
The darkness morphing
Into blinding sunshine

Did fear curl around your neck
Have you bowed
To reputation's shiny exterior
Has pleasing the world consumed
Every facet of your existence

Awaken religious mannequins
Empty as tombs
Dry, brittle bones
Don't you know
There's work to be done

Time is running out
Don't you see it
In front of your eyes
Or are you content
To watch the world burn down?

In Defense Of The Woman About To Be Stoned

You publicly call out her sin
Accusing someone
You've never met
Or walked beside

Your pointed finger
Shooting curses like bullets
I thought we were the rescue team
Not the firing squad

Commissioned as a city on a hill
A beacon in the deep night
Rescuing those stumbling
Toward their demise

Jesus didn't live and resurrect
To modify behavior
But to set souls free
As you look down from the judge's seat

You condemn the darkness
Mock it for not being light
Christ sacrificed Himself for her
So will you throw the first rock?

The Machine

They lured you in
With pretty promises
Of absolute liberation
You decide the truth

You obeyed their creeds
But they chewed you up
Spat you out
And left you to rot

Miraculously you arose
But you learned nothing new
Still singing their songs
Spewing their ideals

What they wanted from the start—
      Another dependent puppet
      Another obedient hound
      Chained to their rhythm

You circle the same mountain
But now you're angry
A rebel without a cause
Leading to death's door every time

Bound to their machinations
And a slave to your passions
Think for yourself
Are you truly enlightened?

The Faults Of Celestial Bodies

You search for signs in the skies
But you'll hear what you want every time
Find anything to blame
Instead of taking responsibility

I never found myself or freedom
Submitting to the stars' directives
Dear fellow human
What makes you any different?

What Would Jesus Do?

Who is this Jesus you speak of
He looks more like *you* every day
He doesn't question your beliefs
Or convict sin—
What's that—
You decide morality
Whatever feels good—
Or not—
I'm sure you mean well
But it's funny how
It's almost as if
Jesus *is* you now
Staring into the mirror
Do you even see a difference
Between this version of Jesus
And yourself

What's it like
Being your own God?

Welcome To The Courtroom

Thus begins my sentencing
I'm dragged before a seething jury
Strangers shouting my offenses—

> Shame for my convictions
> Shame for my skin color
> Shame for my faith

> Shame for loving a man
> With a badge on his chest
> And a golden heart

I either convert myself
Or cower before them
In endless guilt and silence

No matter what I do or say
I can't win
Shame's cycle begs to stay

I risk a glance
At the judge's looming bench
My conscience crushed by accusations

But God sits before me
The One ruling justly
And has the final say

They have no authority here
Despite the merciless jury
God is my judge

The shame they tried
To repackage
Ends here with me.

Broody Vipers

They tried to drain
All the mercy from my marrow
The guilt bypassed the brain
And went straight to the soul
As they lit the pyre
They constructed
For people like me

This is not the kind of world
I want to live in
Where their opinions
Equal moral supremacy
But reek of pride
Shame
And judgment

When did disagreement
Suddenly make you
More holy
Preach tolerance
While you scoff at my beliefs
You made a religion
Of your self-righteous insecurity.

Compliance (Or Else)

I spoke my truth
And they rebutted—
        Wait not like that
No one wants to hear
About the girl
Who couldn't save herself
But sought an *imaginary* God
For deliverance
You only want to hear
My truth
When it's convenient
To your beliefs
And doesn't challenge
Everything you've
Worked so hard
To deconstruct
So let me rephrase
Your doublespeak
When you utter
Speak your truth
You truly mean

Tell me what
I want to hear
Or else.

Jesus Freak

They call me a fool
Yet through every wave of pain
He's the One who stayed.

The One Who Got Away

I sang a haunted song
The melody of a splintered heart
Afflicted with self-hatred
Swaddled in hopelessness

Stumbling through an endless trench
My chant bitter and disappointed—
> *I am not enough*
> *Nothing ever changes*

Yet some distant light found the nerve
To beckon beyond this self-made hell
A calm voice responding
To my cry for help—

I am healing
Love, hope, and peace
Will you trust Me
With your pain and misery

I sing a new song now
I am not the same soul
The girl who wished to perish
Lives on with hope and purpose

I can't give credit to anything else
For the freedom I discovered
Disagree until your dying breath
But here I am as evidence

If you want a sign
Of an available, loving God.

A New Dream

I pray for the harvest
Such a reaping no one has seen
Lost souls stumbling home
Dancing unashamed
In the marvelous light
That I discovered
Outside of man-made traditions
And expectations
Their rules and regulations
Restraining us from God's intentions—
       A relationship between Creator
       And creation
       Father and child

All the Earth is just the beginning
Of a glimmering eternity.

Part 3

Dear God

Letter To God

It's been a while/hasn't it/Quite some time since I've
prayed properly/From faith-filled declarations/to
begging and bargaining/is anyone surprised/my faith
pulls apart at the seams/It was easy to believe/when I
could see Your hand directing blessings/opening
doors/and new horizons/But where are You now/I
ruminate/as I watch good things drop into their
laps/while I collapse into myself/again and again/No
reprieve from this storm/that hasn't let up for years.

How long, Father/I've questioned time after time/The
air remains still and empty/Do You hear me/wailing
on this faithful hardwood floor/consumed by anguish
and panic/How long, Father/until I experience
again/the good gifts You give Your children/How do I
trust You and Your plans/when all paths before me are
bleak and darkened/when there's a gaping precipice/
between my reality/and what You promised.

How quickly I forget/You're the reason I'm
breathing/But even that truth doesn't dismiss these
feelings/Can anger and gratitude exist at the same
time/I wonder/as I scream into blankets/and shake at
the pain coursing up and down my frame.

One day I'll say with confidence/it is well with my
soul/that You are worthy of it all/that I was a good and
faithful servant/that my suffering made me a better
person/and I'll mean it/But until that day/I'll write
these letters/hoping somehow, someway/You could
love an ungrateful daughter.

Blessed Are Those Who Mourn

Want carries a heavy burden
When loss and survival weave your story
The more I *pray* and *have faith*
The more I break down

All I birth are dead things
I can't envision anything
But ashes before me
What does that future hold

But those who mourn
Will receive their due comfort
Be near, Lord
Your children are hurting.

Lullaby For The Weary

They birth babies and career advancements
I conceive double infections
Mental breakdowns
And dreams long buried

Wake me when the nightmare ends
Or if I close my eyes tight enough
Maybe this calamity will be
Nothing more than my imagination

Now I lay me down to sleep
May the dawn's cool touch
Remind me Your mercies
Are as trustworthy as the morning dew.

House Of Cards

Took my gaze
From You
Instead fixated
On these livid swells
This unceasing grief
My resolve dissolving
In the clutches
Of doubt and despair

All the while
The God of everything
Reaches out
And catches
My outstretched hand
Asking me
To believe and trust
In Him again.

By A Thread

Holding on by the hem
Of Your garment
While this tempest dashes me
Against a jagged cliff's edge

But Your faithfulness
Is worth clinging to

Deeper than the waves
That swirl on every side
Higher than the mountain
That refuses to budge

Your endless mercy
Has yet to fail me.

Light Momentary Affliction

Until life came around
And struck me down
Only then did I comprehend
What faith truly meant—

Humming *it is well*
While clumps of hair and tears
Fill your hands
In the shower

Raising your arms
To praise His name
As dizziness threatens
To consume reality

Leaving behind
Everything you worked for
To follow the voice
Of the One who made you

I reconstruct my fragile faith
But one day I'll say
With confidence
You are worthy of it all.

Ground Zero

I proclaimed it as the end—
    A punishment
    Consequences for the life I lived
I see it now for what it was
Mercy somehow
An invitation
To an intentional life
That I wouldn't have found
If not for the
    Breaking
    Burying
    Grieving
    Sowing
    Waiting
    And pruning
You knew
This wouldn't be my demise
But a turnaround
A brand-new day
With brand-new eyes
Fireproof wisdom and courage
To overcome every mountain
That's yet to come.

The Four Winds

Tore through my life
An earthquake shook me
To the marrow
And for the grand finale
Flames devoured
Every inch of my empire

Amidst the chaos
For His voice I listened
Somewhere nearby
He gently whispered
Don't fear the blank page
I'm writing something new.

In The Barren Fields

Living is hard enough
Dreaming feels impossible now
But He tenderly assures me
That's where I step in.

To The Dirt I'll Return

Willpower pushed me so far
But the tank spilled out
Humanity left holes in its wake
And the gasoline spoiled

Mortal strength creates human efforts
Subject to moth and rust
My tenacity celebrated by society
Turned my inner critic into a deity

All these plans
All the scheming
It ends at the grave
Nothing but a hollow dynasty

Anoint me instead
Overflowing with grace
An endless inferno
To build treasures that last.

Resignation Letter

I succumbed to self-reliance
A convenient coping strategy
To survive
> The mental bombardment
> The physical torment
Yet the cycles continued
No matter how hard I tried
I couldn't rely on myself

I have no other place to go
But to my Maker
My ever-present help
But my stubborn nature
Took its sweet time
Arriving there
On my knees
In surrender.

The Plan All Along

The present
Feels like harm
Hopeless
What future
Does this chaos
Even lead to
But that's where
Faith transforms
It's rebuilt from a feeble
House of cards
To an unshakable
Foundation
No longer dependent
 On my wants
 And needs
 Ambition
 And pride
 If I do this right
 Work hard enough
 I'll see it actualize
But instead
Surrendering
To Your plans
For those
Are where
The safety
Hope
And future
Are found.

Vending Machine Deity

You are not the means to my goals
The road I travel to get what I want
You are the Beginning
Middle
And End

Lest I forget
You bestowed my breath
And allotted my days
When will my soul realize
You were always sufficient?

In Defense Of Remaining A Wallflower

But God

It's safer in the dark
The shadows hide my face
       My blatant weakness
       And differences
The things they could pick apart
Reject
Abandon

       (Because they do
       And they did)

I've shown myself
To the world
Twice or thrice
Crawled back to my cave
Bearing memories and pain
Scars on this fragile heart
That You gifted to me

But I can't ignore this tug
Away from my comfort
And if it's Your light
Shining so marvelous
And compelling
Through every crack
In my soul and body

Maybe they won't see me
But You this time.

Security Blanket

Clung to my worry and hurry
As if they could save me
Delay the hounds of reality

I want to trust You entirely
Let the rush and need for control
Slip from clenched hands

At least for now
I've slowed down enough
To sit amongst the birds' songs.

Drifting

Knuckles strained and white
From stubbornly holding on
To my dreams
My way
And expectations
Ironic how the tighter I grip
The more I want to let go
Surrender to the freedom
Of letting You
Be in control
I never knew
         Falling
                  Could be so
                           Freeing.

Allegiance

I've forsaken You
Time after time
Still You leave the ninety-nine
Pull me from the trench
Coax me away from the edge

Great is Your faithfulness
That I've neglected
In exchange for fickle praise
Groveling in compliance
For a tyranny never satisfied

I've sacrificed myself
Long enough on their altar.

Man Of Sorrows

Your dearest companions
Fell asleep while You bled
Deserted at the peak
Of Your suffering
While Your Father looked away

Man of Sorrows
You've held me
Through unending anguish
Could I somehow comfort
You as well?

Birds Of A Feather

Your wings wrapped around me
Through the winding valley
The depths of humanity
I'll follow You into the dark

Even when I surrender
Intertwine with my doubts
Curl up under the ever-frost
And shifting shadows

I can't turn back now
There's nothing for me there
But an open grave
Ever calling my name

Into the ground or unknown—
I'll follow You into the deepest night.

Coexist

Pink sunrises and panic attacks
      Faith and long-suffering
Festivities and grief
      Joy and despair
Anger and thanksgiving
      Content but yearning

You meet me here
In the between.

Even Here

You meet me
With my empty hands
This half-alive body
Bedded in the depths
With nothing to give
But contorted praise
Riddled with anguish
Bitterness pressing in
At the edges—
Please forgive me—
At least I can
Be honest
This turmoil
Doesn't offend You
But rather
You extend
Open arms and hands
With scars on each one

Yes—
Even here
You meet with me.

After All

You lead me through
      The ceaseless pain
      And endings
You gifted this ailing soul
      The courage to persevere
      And hope
      Despite it all
But not without evidence—
      You were there
      You are here
      And You will be ahead
With Your scarred
And outstretched hands
Directing me
      Toward serene emerald pastures
      And lazy streams
Someday I'll reach that haven
      Not near
      Not yet
But promised
Nevertheless.

Tread Lightly

Upon this soil
What we see before us
Is not our home

The strings attaching us
To this beloved Earth
Are the bonds we create
And the legacies we leave

But we are not
Of this world.

Long Live

Bombarded and shell-shocked
Years without reprieve
From hellfire and high waters
Believing there's a light
Beyond this battlefield
Littered with dust and ash

Yet even as I lie here
Waiting for deliverance
My life's refrain remains
Stronger than ever
An unwavering heartbeat
A song amongst the bombs—

Long live the King
Long live the King.

References

Pillar Of Salt: Genesis 19:26

The Former Things: Philippians 3:13-14, Isaiah 43:18

Fork In The Road: Psalms 69:14, Psalms 40:2

In Defense Of The Woman…: John 8:1-11

Welcome To The Courtroom: Psalms 7:8, Psalms 35:23

Broody Vipers: Matthew 12:34

The One Who Got Away: Psalms 40:3

Letter To God: Psalms 6:3, Psalms 13:1, Psalms 35:17

Blessed Are Those Who Mourn: Matthew 5:4

Lullaby For The Weary: Lamentations 3:22-23

House Of Cards: Matthew 14:31

Light Momentary Affliction: 2nd Corinthians 4:17

Hebrews 10:23

The Four Winds: 1 Kings 19:11-12, Isaiah 43:19

Resignation Letter: Psalms 46:1

To The Dirt I'll Return: Psalms 146:3-4, Matthew 6:19-20

Man Of Sorrows: Isaiah 53:3 ESV

The Plan All Along: Jeremiah 29:11

Even Here: Psalms 139: 9-10

Tread Lightly: John 17:14-18

Also By M.M. Bylo

<u>Poetry</u>

The Silent Advocate

Surviving The In-Between

Through The Long, Dark Night

<u>Novels</u>

University

M.M. Bylo is an author residing in the Midwest with her husband and their rescue cat Luna. Professionally speaking, she has written poetry, short stories, and novellas since the age of ten and minored in Creative Writing in college. In reality, all she dreams about is using her love of storytelling and her own experiences to share the love of Christ and encourage others. You can find her snuggled in blankets and fuzzy socks with a book or video game, wandering the outdoors, or trying to convince her perfectionist brain that rest is productive.

www.ingramcontent.com/pod-product-compliance
Lightning Source LLC
Chambersburg PA
CBHW060349050426
42449CB00011B/2892